Meet ... everyone from

JURASSIC WORLD

Jurassic World is in the Pacific Ocean. People come from around the world to see the dinosaurs there.

Owen Grady works with the raptors at Jurassic World. He's very good with animals.

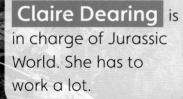

Claire Dearing is in charge of Jurassic World. She has to work a lot.

Vic Hoskins is in charge of all the guards. He likes dinosaurs because they're good hunters.

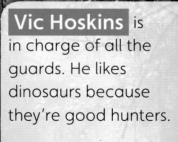

Zach and Gray Mitchell are brothers. Their mum is Claire's sister. Gray loves dinosaurs, but Zach only thinks about girls.

Gray

Zach

The **T. rex** was one of the first dinosaurs at Jurassic World.

The **pterosaurs** live in a glass enclosure. They can fly.

pterosaur enclosure

The **Mosasaurus** is very big. It lives in water.

The **Indominus rex** is a new dinosaur. She has genes from different animals.

Blue is a **raptor**. Raptors are very good at hunting.

Before you read ...
What do you think? Which dinosaur is the most dangerous?

New Words

What do these new words mean? Ask your teacher or use your dictionary.

gene

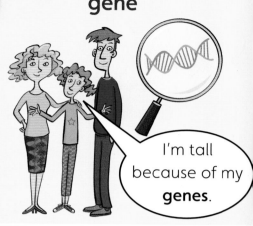

I'm tall because of my **genes**.

change colour

This animal can **change colour**.

glass

They have some **glass**.

in charge of

The teacher is **in charge of** the class.

guard

This man is a **guard**.

gun

Oh no! She's got a **gun**!

hit

Hit it!

hunt

The cat is **hunting**.

kill

Cats **kill** small animals.

waterfall

It's a beautiful **waterfall**.

'Watch out!

Watch out!

Verbs

Present	Past
break	broke
fly	flew
throw	threw

5

CHAPTER 1
A new dinosaur

'Hi, Gray! Hi, Zach!' said Claire Dearing. 'You're very tall now!'

'Of course!' said Zach. Claire was their mum's sister, but she never came to see them.

'This is exciting!' said Gray. 'What are we going to do with you first? Can we see the T. rex?'

'Sorry, boys,' said Claire. 'I have to work today, but you can see all the dinosaurs in Jurassic World.'

Gray and Zach went to see the Mosasaurus. But Zach was on the phone to his girlfriend.

'Watch, Zach!' said Gray.

Suddenly the big Mosasaurus jumped out of the water, and water went everywhere.

'Wow! That was cool!' laughed Zach.

Owen Grady threw some food to the raptors, and the raptors ran to it. Vic Hoskins watched from the top of the enclosure.

'Blue!' Owen shouted. 'Stop!'

One of the raptors looked at Owen. She stopped. Her three sisters stopped too.

'Good girls!' he said.

'They're like dogs, but stronger and faster,' said Vic. 'When can I hunt with them?'

'Never,' said Owen. 'They're too dangerous.'

Claire was at Jurassic World's newest enclosure. She didn't like going to see the dinosaurs. She was frightened of them.

'We're going to open this in three weeks,' she said to a guard. 'Are there any problems?'

'The Indominus rex is the cleverest and most dangerous dinosaur at the park,' he said. 'There are always problems.'

'Maybe Owen Grady needs to look at the enclosure,' Claire thought.

Owen went to meet Claire at the new enclosure. 'What's in there?' he asked.

'This is the Indominus rex,' said Claire. 'The old dinosaurs aren't exciting for people these days. So we made a new dinosaur with the genes of different animals. She's like a T. rex, but she's bigger and cooler.'

'What's not cool about a T. rex?' asked Owen. He looked in the enclosure.

'It's easy to see her,' said Claire. 'She's very big.'

'She's not there,' Owen said slowly.

'Oh no!' said Claire. 'Did she get out?'

CHAPTER 2
'Close the park!'

Owen and some guards walked slowly into the enclosure. The guards were very frightened.

'I can't see her,' said one guard quietly.

'No, she isn't here,' said his friend.

Suddenly something moved in front of them.

'It's her! Watch out!' Owen shouted.

Everyone started to run. But the guard was too slow. The Indominus killed him. Then she ran out of the enclosure.

'Close the park!' Claire shouted into her phone.

'Why couldn't we see her?' thought Owen. 'Which animal has she got genes from?'

Zach and Gray were in a glass car, and there were dinosaurs all around them.

'This is great!' said Zach.

'Sorry! The park is closing now,' said the car's computer. 'Please go back.'

'But it isn't late,' said Zach. 'Let's stay here. It's more exciting!'

Now they were the only people in the park.
'It's better with no one here,' said Zach.
'I don't like it,' said Gray. 'We need to go.'
There was a noise behind them.
'What's that?' asked Gray.

Something big hit the car. It was the Indominus!
'Help!' shouted Gray.
'It's OK,' said Zach. 'This car's very strong. She can't break it.'
The Indominus threw the car, and the glass broke.
'Yes, she can!' shouted Zach. 'Run!'

The boys ran. There was a waterfall in front of them. 'Jump!' said Zach.

'I can't!' said Gray.

But the Indominus was not far behind. They jumped.

'You did it, Gray!' laughed Zach.

They started to run back.

'We have to find Zach and Gray!' Claire shouted to Owen.

'Look!' said Owen. 'It's the Indominus!'

'She's running into the pterosaurs' enclosure!' said Claire.

The Indominus broke the glass of the enclosure, and the pterosaurs flew out.

'Run, Claire!' shouted Owen.

CHAPTER 3
Raptor genes

Zach and Gray were back near the Mosasaurus. There were a lot of unhappy people there. The park wasn't open and they wanted to go home.

'Watch out!' someone shouted.

There was a pterosaur near them, and it had a woman in its feet!

Soon there were pterosaurs everywhere.

'Run, Zach!' shouted Gray.

A pterosaur flew at Claire and Owen. Owen hit it away, but it came back.

'Get off me!' shouted Owen.

Claire found Owen's gun. 'I can do this!' she thought.

She killed the pterosaur. Owen was OK!

Zach and Gray saw her. 'Wow! Is that Claire?' said Zach.

Claire ran to them. 'You're OK too!' she said happily.

Hoskins had an idea. 'We need to hunt the Indominus with your raptors,' he said to Owen.

'No!' said Owen. 'They're too dangerous. You know that.'

'We're doing this!' said Hoskins. 'Are you going to help or not?'

Owen and the raptors started to hunt the Indominus. Hoskins and his guards came behind them.

Suddenly the raptors saw the Indominus.

'Go, Blue!' said Owen.

But Blue and the other raptors waited. The Indominus made noises, and the raptors answered.

'They're talking,' thought Owen. 'The Indominus has some raptor genes!'

Then the raptors started to kill the guards.

'Run!' shouted Owen. 'The Indominus is in charge now!'

'The Indominus has raptor genes. Did you know?' Owen asked Hoskins angrily.

'Of course!' laughed Hoskins. 'But my best idea was the genes to change colour. No one can see her when she's hunting!'

'Wow! The Indominus was your idea!' said Owen.

Suddenly a raptor came near Hoskins.

'It's OK,' he said to her. 'I'm a hunter too. We're friends.'

But the raptor didn't want a friend. She wanted dinner. She jumped on him.

CHAPTER 4
A very cool dinosaur

'You've got us now,' Owen said quietly. 'Clever girl, Blue!'

The raptors were all around Owen, Claire and the boys.

'The Indominus is coming!' said Claire.

Blue moved nearer to Owen.

'It's OK, Blue,' he said. He put his gun down.

Blue stood between Owen and the Indominus. The big dinosaur hit Blue away angrily. But the other raptors jumped on the Indominus.

The Indominus was too strong for the raptors.

'We need something bigger than the raptors,' said Gray.

'I have an idea!' shouted Claire.

She ran to the T. rex enclosure and opened the door. She had a light in her hand. The T. rex ran after her light.

'The T. rex is bigger!' Claire said to Gray.

The T. rex ran at the Indominus. But the Indominus hit the T. rex again and again. The T. rex couldn't stand up.

'No!' said Zach. 'The Indominus is going to win!'

'It's OK!' said Owen quietly. 'Blue is coming back.'

   With Blue's help, the T. rex was soon on
her feet again, and she threw the Indominus
onto the road near the Mosasaurus.
   The Mosasaurus jumped out of the water.
And when it went back under, it had the
Indominus with it.

'They did it!' said Gray happily. 'The raptors and the T. rex!'

'And you helped them, Claire!' said Owen.

Claire laughed. 'The T. rex is a very cool dinosaur!' she said.

THE END

IT'S ALL IN THE GENES

cytos

What is genetic engineering?

Scientists can change the genes of a plant or animal. They can give it genes from a different plant or animal. Maybe they want to make a plant bigger, or better at living in very hot or cold places. Maybe they want to stop a disease in an animal.

Scientists made this **new onion**. People don't cry when they cut it.

Mammoths are extinct. Some scientists think that mammoths can live again, with the help of genetic engineering and genes from elephants.

INDOMINUS REX

The scientists at Jurassic World made the Indominus rex with genes from different dinosaurs and animals.

She had **cuttlefish** genes, so she could change colour.

She had **pit viper** genes, so she could see in the dark.

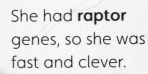

She had **raptor** genes, so she was fast and clever.

She had **T. rex** genes, so she was big and strong.

What do these words mean? Find out.

scientist   plant   disease
extinct   elephant

What do you think? Is genetic engineering a good idea?

After you read

1 True (✓) or False (✗)? Write in the box.

a) Claire was frightened of the Indominus. ✓

b) The Indominus broke the boys' glass car. ✓

c) The pterosaurs broke the glass of their enclosure. ✓

d) Owen killed a pterosaur. ✗

e) The Indominus had some raptor genes. ✓

f) The Indominus was Claire's idea. ✗

g) Hoskins was friends with the raptors. ✗

h) The T. rex and the Indominus were friends. ✗

2 Answer the questions.

a) Where does the Mosasaurus live?

b) Why could no one see the Indominus in her enclosure?

c) Who wanted to stay in the park after it closed?

d) Which two people jumped down a waterfall?

e) Which dinosaurs hunted the Indominus?

f) Who opened the door for the T. rex?

g) Where did the T. rex throw the Indominus?

Where's the popcorn?
Look in your book.
Can you find it?

Puzzle time!

1 Complete the sentences.

a) The Indominus can c **h a n g e** c _ _ _ _ _ , so
people can't see her.

b) She is brown when she is in her e _ _ _ _ _ _ _ _ _ .

c) She is green when she is in the p _ _ _ .

d) She is grey when it is n _ _ _ _ _ .

a)

b)

c)

d)

2 Write the words.

```
          ¹g
           u
    ²G  L  a  S  S
  ³       r        ⁴
   ⁵      d
 ⁶
```

3 True (✓) or False (✗)? Read and follow the lines.

a) The raptor has got more food than the pterosaur. [✗]

b) The pterosaur eats more than the T. rex. [✗]

c) The Mosasaurus eats the most. [✓]

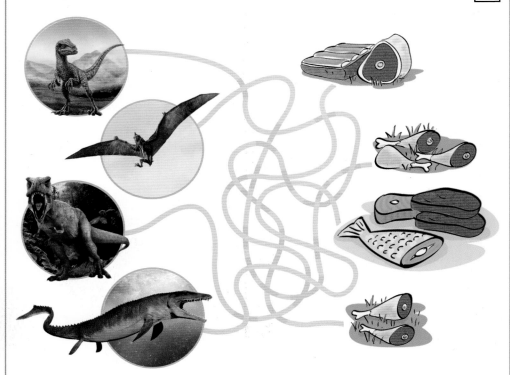

4 Answer the questions. Then ask your friends.

Would you like to:

		Yes	No
a)	be a guard at Jurassic World?	✓	
b)	hunt with raptors?		
c)	jump down a waterfall?		
d)	go in a glass car?		
e)	change the colour of your hair?		